Mermaids of Albuquerque

Saint Julian Press
Poetry

BOOKS BY THE AUTHOR

Bird Light

The Patron Saint of Cauliflower

Martini Tattoo

The Economist's Daughter

The Family on Beartown Road

The Hypothetical Girl

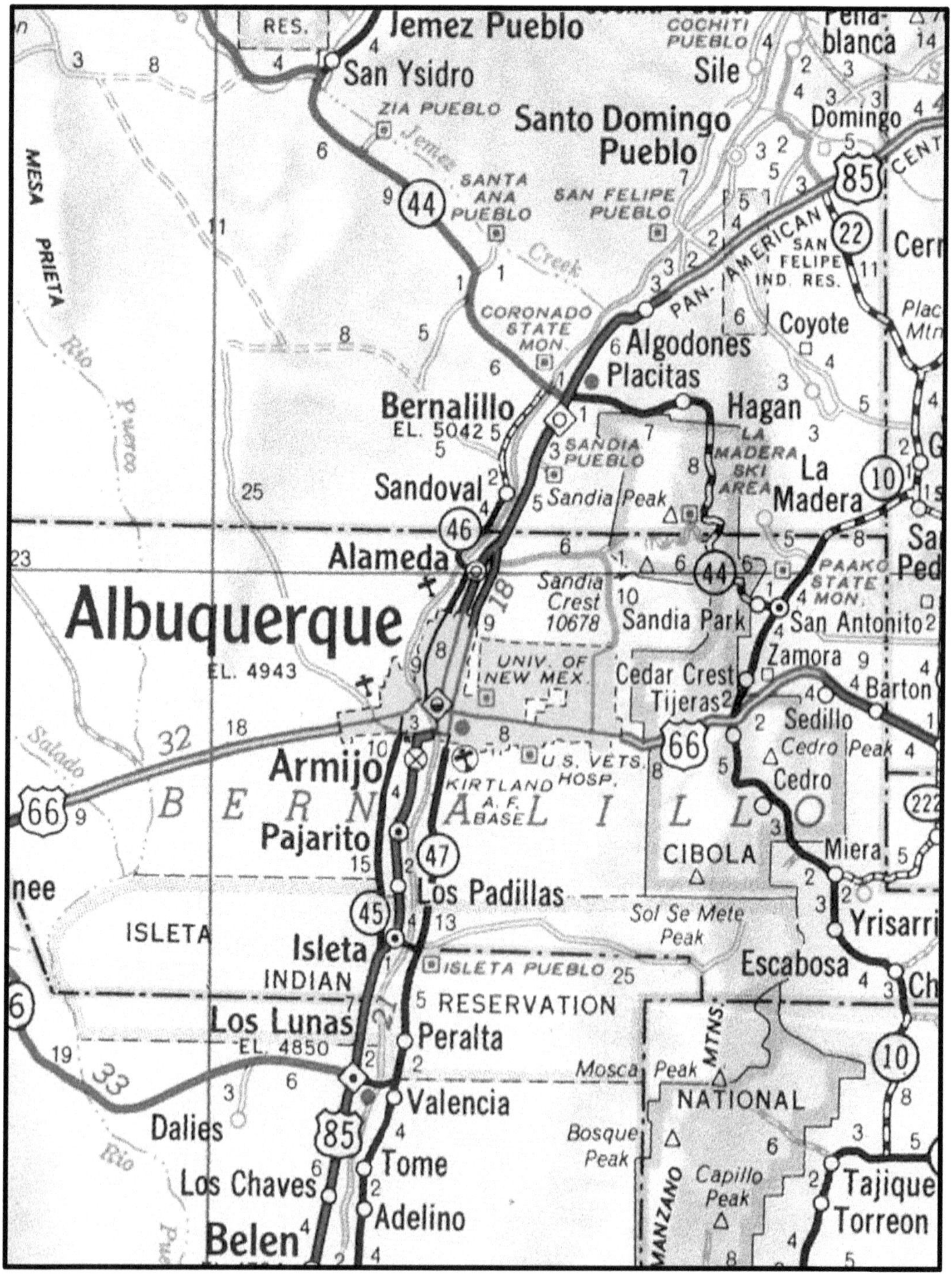
Jemez Pueblo
San Ysidro
ZIA PUEBLO
Jemez
Santo Domingo Pueblo
COCHITI PUEBLO
Sile
Peña Blanca
Domingo
SANTA ANA PUEBLO
SAN FELIPE PUEBLO
MESA PRIETA
Creek
PAN-AMERICAN
CENT
SAN FELIPE IND. RES.
Cerr
Coyote
Plac Mtn
CORONADO STATE MON.
Algodones
Placitas
Hagan
Rio Puerco
Bernalillo
EL. 5042
SANDIA PUEBLO
LA MADERA SKI AREA
La Madera
Sandoval
Sandia Peak
Alameda
PAAKO STATE MON.
Sandia Crest 10678
Sandia Park
San Antonito
Albuquerque
EL. 4943
UNIV. OF NEW MEX.
Zamora
Cedar Crest
Barton
Tijeras
Sedillo
Cedro Peak
Cedro
Salado
Armijo
U.S. VETS. HOSP.
KIRTLAND A.F. BASE
BERNALILLO
Pajarito
CIBOLA
Miera
Los Padillas
Sol Se Mete Peak
Yrisarri
ISLETA
Isleta
ISLETA PUEBLO
INDIAN
RESERVATION
Escabosa
Los Lunas
EL. 4850
Peralta
Mosca Peak
MTNS.
NATIONAL
Valencia
Dalies
Bosque Peak
Tome
Los Chaves
MANZANO
Capillo Peak
Tajique
Adelino
Torreon
Belen
Rio Puerco

Mermaids of Albuquerque

Poems

by

Elizabeth Cohen

SAINT JULIAN PRESS
HOUSTON

Published by
SAINT JULIAN PRESS, Inc.
2053 Cortlandt, Suite 200
Houston, Texas 77008

www.saintjulianpress.com

ISBN-13: 978-1-955194-39-6
Library of Congress Control Number: 2024944563

Cover Art Credit: "Sea Goddess" by Alexandra Eldridge

CONTENTS

IV. Speaking the Garden

"Sadness can run a mermaid aground on the mudflats of despair. But her tears make the ocean deeper."

—Margot Datz, *A Survival Guide for Landlocked Mermaids*

Mermaids
of
Albuquerque

I.
The Art of Coming Home Again

Guadalupe Trail

I could say I come
from dust, from rocks

Potatoes, centuries of bloody
fingers, tatting lace

I could say I come a thousand years
wandering in a desert

Russian steppes, pograms
death camps, bone yards

I could say I come
from candles

reversed mirrors
glasses of wine

I could say I come from
a Purple heart, moldy feet

in the jungles of the Philippines
from decoded enemy messages

crossword puzzles, recipes for soup
I could say I come from laundry

washed in a bathtub in Cleveland,
the American labor movement

I could say I come from heat
I could say I come from ice

all these things are true
but opening my heart's book, I say

I come from 8209 A Guadalupe Trail
the place I lost and grew teeth

planted striped zucchini
climbed a rickety windmill

learned a Torah parsha,
buried dogs, cats, generations

of chickens, one goat,
infinite goldfish

I come from a sanctuary
under a fallen tree on the irrigation ditch

where I came to see every person
under a tree is drinking shade

every person is water
feeding a tree

I'm from the nectar
of Guadalupe Trail

from long thin scratches
from Russian Olives

an invasive species introduced
in the late 1800s, run wild

that's me, an imported
barefoot wild girl

swung many dozen times
over that ditch on a knotted rope

we are all the places we began
and if you leave and return

you might walk someday
on top of your own footprints

you might hear distant barking
from across the decades

of that last dog
crushed by a hit-and-run on 4th Street

still calling for you
to save her

Re-Entry

It’s a cherry bomb
lollipop, coloring book

Saturday morning cartoon
New Mexico moon.

Meanwhile, the ghosts of dogs
are barking; what’s left of family

A flock of smeary chemtrails
even the stars, of course, are long dead

Flashing their corpse eyes
down from their graves

Returning’s no river picnic,
no triumphant slide into home

It’s work, re-entry, reclaiming home
an astronaut described

The sky— light pink,
shifting to deeper pink,

Then blooming red.
“what you realize,” he said,

“Is you’re looking
from the inside of a fireball

Being ripped apart”
returning requires moxy,

Bravado, pluck,
a posse of guardian angels

Eventually gift baskets will arrive,
delivering shovelfuls of rainbow

Super blooms, waterfall canyons
A pink water balloon moon

That bumps up against the mountains
pops, and showers the sky in golden light

everything is opposite

how the desert breaks
into a sweat at night

how the silk of sand
is knotted with burrs

how certain butterflies in Africa
 can poison a cat

how they say they found
"buckling" water on the moon

edible gold flowers
white chocolate chips

grape nuts
(which are neither grapes or nuts)

how, before his death, my father said he
was abducted in Bolivia for seeding revolt

how yours, a scientist in Michigan, said he
controlled weather by speaking in tongues

Chachalaca

Anarchist, rebel, Chachalaca,
the bird websites say

you should be three hundred
miles south, yet here you are

screaming in this dandelion bright
Aspen grove, beside the Jemez River.

Look at you, strutting, flitting,
big as a chicken.

Did nobody tell you?
This is Dove country.

Bushels of Grackles
have been spotted here

along with an occasional
posse of geese, but you?

This could be some portent
of world disorder, collapse,

avian confusion, or worse,
but Chachalaca, I'm going with lucky.

I won't take your picture,
post the date,

your GPS coordinates,
or tell a soul about our encounter.

There is no explaining this meeting
here on the back page of the world

so far from our usual roosts;
me, on the couch where I curl

with my dog, you, in the lantana
gardens of the Tamaulipan brush

where it's said
your raucous morning songs

rile everyone,
even waken the dead.

poem with six Mourning Doves, a Roadrunner and a milk carton

any morning will tell you
what night left behind

darkness still humming
beneath the trees

smelling of the dreaming
of animals

soil exhaling
all that goes on underground

(the pulling of worms,
water funneling, deep to deeper)

Mourning Doves arrive
from their scrub nests

to strut and preen
they can't help it

they're so happy
good moods with wings

any morning will remind you
fresh chances lie ahead

brand new and do-overs
sunlight cartwheels

the fence
kicking the shadows

back to their beds
come on out, see

birds in groups
birds in pairs

birds on solitary missions
their appetites reeling

them through the dawn
they buy in on the idea

of insects, while the insects
buy in on the orange strands

of yucca, honey buried
in the yawning

squash blossoms
they're excited by the worms

evicted by pre-dawn rain
and garbage day

their favorite day
the sigh and groan

rounding the corner
hefting excess

sluffing bottles
that clink and toast

in the scrambledust
Those Mourning Doves

watch for spillage—
a dozen or so soggy beans

a smiling rind of watermelon
a Roadrunner

pecks at the waxy corpse
of a milk carton

flattened in the gutter
any morning will tell you

the world is just dying
 to do better than yesterday

that Roadrunner
in her speckled cape

and brown stilettos
nocturnal meanderings behind her

digs into the wreckage
steadfastly seeking a prize

the honey bees

chose the puddle
by the leaky hose
to party, then spread out
all afternoon
drifting in the gazanias

later, they slow dance
with the queens of the night
in the golden barrels
proving happiness
can be a drunken festival

later, partied out, they'll retire
to the rafters
and their intricate palace
of sweets

a honeybee brain
is the size
of a poppy seed
and they only live
for a month

obviously, they must
make the most of it
before they turn
everything over
to the next generation
who'll rise up, singing
and dancing as if they
are the first bees ever born
to sway into the golden hour
the flowering

morning glories

when everything else is dying
they bask in the early sun

open their arms
with wild abandon

then close their bright eyes
to nap in the afternoons

they'll do this right up
to the first hard frost

optimistic as beautiful
letters sent during wars

as if nothing bad
has ever happened in the world

no child stolen
from her mother

dragged into a dark tunnel
or left naked and dead

on the same road
she walked daily

with books and a bag lunch
to get to school

Skunk Forecast

scurrier, bandit, little sneak
crisscrossing rock
white stripe of day
slapped onto night

mist fills
the spot in the morning
slinks under creosote
then changes its mind
pivots west toward the river

it's October.
the vitex tree ambers
done with all that drifty blue
tomatoes drop their green skirts
and blush

everything knows
it's time to shift, move on
make space
for what's coming next

I'm the seven of cups,
the coffee grounds in the mug
predicting high wind
a twenty percent chance
of afternoon rain

as dusk strolls up
I put my money
on another night cameo
a ten percent chance
I'll see her again.

I'm a good prognosticator
this time she brings her kits,
a batch of dash marks
who see me, then sprint
to their sweet place
their safe house
tucked under mine

II.
This Was Once a Sea

this was once a sea

creep snail
wave coral
fish bones
broke rocks
glacier-kicked
waiting
forever for high tide

an ocean dies
but leaves
its glossary
sharkfin, trilobite
seagrass, sargassum
stamp and scramble
on mesa back
like names engraved
on Inscription Rock

once this
was a society
but like the Olmecs
it vanished

you can smell
the afterlife
cave-breath
monster breath
hibbertopterus lamsfelli
who trolled
this former sea
sweep feeding
leaving behind
its Roman sword
its rows of spindly
segmented legs

Mermaids of Albuquerque

Imagine them sunbathing on the shore of the Sandias,
long locks rustling like Mexican feather grass.
Later, down in the bosque, flipping iridescent
tails skyward, diving into the acequia.

Once a month, they go to Tingley Beach to feed the geese,
bathe in moonlight, listen to the opera of animals
at the zoological park, lowing to children
they know they'll never see again.

The mermaids of Albuquerque understand.
Once they had a great sea, waves and particles
that rose and fell, tided and king tided, exhaling weeds
and shell onto ancient beaches, luring ancestors of birds.

Once they had currents, grottos, spin-cycling whirlpools.
They fanned themselves with lacy bryozoans.
Collected coin size brachiopods like souvenirs.
Swam through whole apartment complexes of fish.

Now the mermaids visit Bone Spring cemetery,
a limestone catalogue of the last mass extinction.
Bivalve clams and those brachiopods stamp the headstones.
Sea urchin and nautiloid spirit the cliffs.

The mermaids of Albuquerque sing to their departed sea
dried into a circuitry of salted slot canyons,
long-limbed black mesas, peppered with ash.
To the alkaline ledger of species, keeping track.

Now truck stops inlet the basin. Diesel-hunting schools
of long haulers congregate, freighted with vegetables,
electronics, and human cargo, too. Beating hearts,
tied to one another, baled, like hay.

The mermaids of Albuquerque sing to their captivity.
They've witnessed every genre of vanishing.
They swim the asphalt interstate, passing miles
of pumpjacks, greedily milking the blood past.

The mermaids sing to ghosts of woolly mammoths,
to hidden caverns of copper and bats. They know none
of this has to do with them. Not the microchipped
desert, the fire-scorched hills, the anemic Rio Grande,

Pecos, Gila and Las Animas, waterways veined
with unstable isotopes, plastic shopping bags,
discarded tires, and beer cans, astride rock cliffs
imprinted with extinct, cartilaginous fish.

The mermaids of Albuquerque swim the river, rigged
south to capture refugees. Sing to dreamers
who survived borderlands. They recognize it: the world
changes without sentiment, leaving pieces behind.

Look at what has survived the defection of those waters.
The dried seabed scuttles with scorpions, slithering snakes.
It's not hard to imagine their lobster and seasnake ancestors,
great underwater creatures, silently paddling the expanse.

III.
They Were Mermaids

The Ghost of Willa Cather at Tastee Freeze

I'm with orphan Jim and Antonia
in the gold-tipped treetops of Nebraska,
at Tastee Freeze, off Rio Grande
in the Village of Los Ranchos, 1975

The river, a sand pit
in the rising heat, whistles softly
sweat pulls across my face
while in Nebraska
a scrim of ice forms on the lake

Tastee Freeze has a new promotion
the Oreo Soft Serve shake
which tastes like everything good
in the world, but makes my teeth ache

The ghost of Willa Cather floats
beside me at the picnic table—
she's just back from a visit
with the ghosts of Red Cloud
at Mesa Verde, by the white
striped escarpments, tiny houses
tucked into cliffs like the caves
housing Antonia's family

Willa and I watch locusts
make parabolas in the weeds
I swat a few ants, a horsefly
settles on my shoe, rubs its legs
I'm in the heat, I'm in the cold
I'm deep in both, riding waves
of sugar, slipping back and forth
across a century, toggling
Nebraska and New Mexico

It's my fourth trip with Willa
my third on my bike down Alameda
I'm five chapters in, thirty years away
from a giant crack in the world

Spoiler Alert: Antonia's dad kills himself
in chapter fourteen
Spoiler Alert: the Oreo Soft Serve Shake
might freeze your brain
Spoiler Alert: Tastee Freez will go out of business
and then be brought back in 2004
Spoiler Alert: the planet will shift on its axis
when the century turns

Willa, Antonia and I will swim
to the surface of that moment
to see what's left of the world—

how winter forgets its place in the seasons
how water forgets where and when to fall

On the Last Will and Testament of Doña Elena Gallegos

And I declare that I was born
a ghost child whose parents fled
the pueblo revolt
only to return as a ghost family

And I declare there was no mention
of my family in the census of 1693
And there was no mention of our cattle
in the cattle distribution census of 1697

And I declare that I had
no birth certificate
and there was no mention
of my existence anywhere

And I declare that in 1600, I married
the French sailor Santiago Gurule'
who had traveled the world
tough as a square-rigged galleon

And I declare my husband
brought his thick arms painted
with bright birds
his scarred knuckles and gold
to ask for my hand

And I declare he'd changed his name
after an ill-fated expedition to Mexico
and was seventeen years older than me
and I didn't speak a word of French

And I declare that after we married
I was born into the known world
my name appearing on deeds
and documents regarding cattle

And I declare when my husband
died, I changed my name back
and was born again to myself
to the name I never had

And I declare I took ownership
of a land grant of seventy thousand acres
And I declare I took ownership
of my own livestock brand

And I declare I worked that land
all my living days with my brother Philip
and my son Antonio

And I declare that I leave to Antonio
the house of my residence
with its drainage and a plot of land

And to my brother
I leave three Galician horses
two yoke of oxen, twelve mares
two mules, two colts,
one two-year-old and the other, one

And I declare I leave two silk shirts
a cloak, a pink mantle, a silk shawl
a petticoat and a silver pendant
to my granddaughter, Manuela

And to this world, I unofficially declare
a posthumous establishment of an open space
named for me, for the enjoyment
and pleasure of future people
born with their names attached
whose children will be born with their names
and birthdates, too

And I command that this, my Last Will
be kept and fulfilled, although my name herein
is unsigned, not because I have no name
but because I do not know how to write

And I unofficially declare that my lands
shall hereafter be known by this name
I could not write, a name that will someday
be inscribed on signs and maps
and in history books

I am Doña Elena Gallegos
and I believe loyally and truly
in the Mystery of the Holy Trinity—
Father, son and Holy Spirit

And I profess that I wish to live and die
confessing this truth

And I declare I have commanded
that this, my legacy and my name
like my last will, be kept and forever
fulfilled. And I do not sign this document
but I declare that it, like my name
and birthdate, is official and, now
forever and eternally, mine

The Ghost of Mary Elizabeth Jane Colter
Visits the Site of the Former Alvarado Hotel

Days of busy wind
trundle former Route 66
depositing a layer
of mesa dust
dust of caldera and wash

That's where you might
see a wisp of sand glitter
meshed with castoff cups
the cellophane skins
of American Spirits

That's Mary Elizabeth Jane Colter
with everything missing—
T-Square, scale ruler
compass, triangle
signature calico
brooch at the neck

Sweeping away alluvial
residue, spinning
along the sidewalk
sweeping in sharp bursts
sweeping in circles

Sweeping away
at the sidewalk
that fronted her gothic stop
on American rails
sweeping the entry to
a Fred Harvey lodging
sweeping any settled detritus
any remaining atom
of what was

The ghost of Frank Lloyd Wright
who invented the future
spirits far away over falling water
while Mary Elizabeth Jane Colter
re-invented the past
at Hermit's Rest, Hopi House
Lookout Studio
Desert View Watchtower
the spot she is sweeping
home of the decimated
Alvarado Hotel
is now replaced by an urban facsimile
transit hub, a quotation collecting
mica dust, cans, newspaper pages that float
and tarry like the homeless, along this curb

She's a fastidious
mother, sweeping the grave
of her beautiful child
gone, it's red tile parapets
steel-stooled lunch counters
gone, peppermint barber poles
the tawny hued
Mission Revival arch

It can be hard to mourn
when authentic bones are gone
but on certain wind-filled days
you can see spinning dust
sweep in circular rotations
rising at times into tiny devils
of dust, pink storms that prickle
pockmark, sting

Sweeping as if someday she might
recover some small memento:
a nut, a bolt, a bright chip of tile

The Lungs of Carrie Wooster Tingley

She stepped off the train
to breathe

and the scent was piñon
and petrichor

mesquite and roasted chile
river exhaling river

mountain exhaling mountain
pueblo breath, pottery breath

breath of mesa
high desert breath

volcano breath
breath of ancient sea

It was 1911 and Arizona
was just too far

so Carrie Wooster stepped
off the train at the Alvarado Hotel

trading lungs filled
with Ohio and tuberculosis

for the thin dry air
of the Rio Grande valley

stepped into the long pink
shadow of the Sandia Mountains

then walked to the river
of ducks and striped turtles

noses lifting
from muddy shallows

small islands
surfacing

With her mother, Carrie Wooster
stepped off the train

into Albuquerque
and there married Clyde Tingley

together they gifted a pond
and a hospital for children

gifted a world of good
like holiday packages

to a place
she never intended to go

Carrie Wooster, a dying girl
stepped off a train

and breathed her life
into Albuquerque

where she had stopped to breathe
and breathing there was what saved her

IV.
Speaking the Garden

Sunflowers

I'm here in the country of sunflowers
bent over from the weight

of their own beauty, unfurling
their bright flags, signaling departure

summer has
given them too much

sunshine to carry
and now they are dying

from the burden
of all that light

I think I must speak
fluent sunflower

my mind also heavy with
the surplus beauty of being alive

moving into my autumn now
I hear them and answer

their exhausted yellow voices
feel their crisp tilting, their surrender

Cherry Tomatoes

1.
I'm eating my children this morning,
I couldn't resist

their blushing faces
sweet little souls

red lanterns waving
from across the yard.

One-by-one, I let them
burst and light up my tongue

with the taste of sunjuice,
deluge, drought, dew

sprinkler rainbow— all the dances
of summer.

I choose first the bright-faced
and ruddy.

Later, I'll choose shy blushers,
hiding behind the scenes.

I'll ferret and ambush
them, stash them

in my bucket
see how much they've grown.

Such troopers, such achievers,
not a slacker among them.

I've been cheering them on
since the day

they came into the world,
tiny as raindrops

determined nothing
would slow them,

(even the tossed stones
of wild hail in May).

look now at how well-rounded
and decent they've become.

They're handling the heat wave
--four days of three digits--

like bosses, never once
falling or faltering.

Sometimes, at daybreak
when I shower them with the hose

I think I hear them drinking
brightening, swelling

proving something good
will come of them.

I'm an equal opportunity consumer,
I even eat the injured

and now I'll eat this littlest one
attacked by a bird

I do not discriminate.
Confession:

I'd chew them, swallow,
digest them all

even if they weren't
such rock stars,

with their heirloom pedigrees
(Sungold! Midnight Snack!)

Each time, before I
put one in my mouth,

I hold it between my fingers
just to see the way it glows.

Such beautiful darlings,
bright garden marbles,

roaring with life.

2.
When I was small and disobeyed
my mother used to say,

"I brought you into this world
and I'll take you out."

I found it the strangest
remonstration of love,

this peculiar threat
that at any moment,

for any random reason,
she might decide

to stuff me back inside her.
But this summer

I finally get it, as I
swallow the fruits of my labor,

these little ones that have done
so well for themselves.

Despite the grasshoppers
and disrespecting wind

they've persevered,
become these extraordinary

tender, scarlet planets,
gelatinous, fleshy

liquid; tiny miracles
that explode in my mouth.

I'm mom and midwife,
I'm Titus Cronus

in that scary painting by Goya,
Saturn, his mouth agape,

a toothy bedlam,
swallowing innocence.

I'm their mother and mine.
I brought them into the world,

and now I'm taking them back.

winded

who gave you permission to run
around the house

go up on the roof, yelling
& screaming, make a mess

of the garden, throwing yourself
mercilessly at the sunflowers

who bow down
like lunatics

followers of a cult
of tremblers

watching you arrest
the development of the infant peas

then go all in and destabilize
the woodpile like a revolutionary

but your violence in the forest
dwarfs these crimes

there, you kneecap trees,
toss their limbs into roads

after you've left, strange quiet arrives
you did something big and now it's done

who wouldn't admire
that fierce way you stirred up

the loose skin of the mesa
bloodied the riverbank

confused the dogs
who could not determine

which way to bark
back at you

that sound you made
is that sound of things

breaking, cracking
broken souls of ladders

carports, garbage bins
briefly taught to fly

what hubris, your sixty-two-mile
per-hour ego, the world

is your bitch, your mare running in
in circles, your pummeled slave

laundry thief
abductor of leaves

unleashing and exploding
this ordered world, loading up

the arroyos with plastic bags
just tell us who invited you

to come here and pour yourself
a bowl of Albuquerque

top it with pollen
and candy wrappers

then leave the airport dunes
fancy-swirled

clouds above, similarly
fashioned— after you're gone

it's arresting; "windswept"
becomes artisan

ornate, bespoke
ridiculously fancy

after you come
and beat it down

the world is gorgeously
destroyed

teensy purple seedlets
flower trash in gutters

glowing, so many diamonds
of shiny, invincible sand

Eclipse

It was black with a neon orange penumbra
that became a hat
which became a cap
which became a yarmulke
which became a beard
which became a chip on a shoulder
which became a nibble
which became a shift of light
which became nothing.
And then became everything.
All over again.

Eclipse on the Eve of War

Then the earth swung open its gate
(the moon slipping in)

Then the sun rushed up
(plowing the field with bright)

Then the moon made a long speech
(for a body so comparatively small)

Then the day winced
(which made the night come back)

Then shadows dropped their jaws
(exposing their wide O mouths)

Then tanks rolled forward
(it rained missiles; it rained fire)

A nightmare like a sparkler
(electric yellow sprung with blue)

Crackling when lit
(then left you wondering where, why)

How quickly a beautiful moon dance can end
(It was just a blink of dark, after all)

War Followed by Ring of Fire Eclipse, on Your Daughter's 25th Birthday

Your daughter's birthday
is wearing a deathmask.
It's been denied water,
crowned with blood thorns,
starved in dark places,
underground.

If you could, you'd birth her
on any day other than this
unlucky date, sliced out
of the calendar,
marked for siege.

(And with that tiny girl
weeping on her street of fire.)

Just take this ruined day back,
trade it in for a hurricane,
earthquake, brush fire,
anything but this siege of souls.

How fortuitous her birthday
might have seemed
just a week later, the sun
on a dimmer switch, toggling
back and forth, wearing a gold crown.

What do you want for your birthday?
The question hereafter
locked and loaded.
Mothers in black dresses,
mourning, despising cake,
ice cream, streamers,
all those too bright balloons.

Labor Arbitrator

"Plant marigolds around the edges,"
my father said. Like a hoop of fire
they'll cast a protection spell,
guard the garden, keep intruders out.

"Plant tomatoes in the rain.
Rain is good for planting everything."

So we planted our beds, big and small,
side-by-side, in drizzle which turned
mudfest, our caked shoes at the door.

My mother canned and froze
the whole of it, feeding us
back the summer
all fall and winter.
Feeding back plums
from the courtyard tree.
Pies. Jam. Turnovers.

He got me a tiny hoe and shovel,
told me stories while I dug.
"They're fighting at the copper mine,"
he reported. "Anaconda."

My plot was small but mighty.
Standing inside it, I pictured
saber-wielding pirates in a shiny cave.
Anaconda, an opal-eyed snake,
separating the sides. Mining people
had called him in, my father said,
"to listen to both sides."

There are always two sides.
It all made sense.

He pointed with a stick
at the ground outside the marigolds.
"Worms and ladybugs
are helpers, too."
Then he pointed to the sky
which was sobbing,
"That makes everything happen."

Rain, bugs, vegetables,
a flower fence. Underground,
in Arizona, a fight raging
with a sacred snake.

In the midst of their warring,
these rough warriors
summoned my father,
with his tattered briefcase
and receding hairline,
thick glasses, tan trench.

I watched him point
at the ground, then the sky.
He was a man who understood
the many sides of things.

He was gone a week, came home
rumpled and tired
and I knew why.

Somewhere in Arizona, my father
cast a protection spell,
made warring sides agree.

At the dinner table he said,
"everyone was satisfied.
Pass the potatoes."

We'd grown those too,
he and I, planted them in rain,
and they were delicious.

Night of the Cover Bands

it is June
  and we are not 21

we were not supposed to take the car
  we are not wearing our seatbelts

we are waiting for not Joe Strummer
  not Debbie Harry, not Morrissey

their counterfeit voices
    to rise beneath the frantic licking guitar

they are not our heroes
    but we are not us yet either

you, with your eyeliner and safety pin earring
    me, in my white wig and stilettos

we both know
    these are temporary disguises

what we do not know is you will go on
    to invent an alternative form of energy

I will go on to teach poetry
    to nursing students in upstate New York

yet here we are in this, our prelude
    you, with your cherry cigar

me, wobbling on those stilettos,
    oh how much we want to be something

anything, as long as it's shiny
our throats fill with reticent whoop and howl

later the police will pull us over
for that dead taillight

I'll toss my white wig and those shoes
over the Corrales bridge

we'll run barefoot crookedly
toward dawn, an amber freight train

pulling in to take us away
from that night and all the beautiful forgery

too bad we didn't know yet
that you would climb Everest

and I'd dervish in Prague
that someday we'd have happy children

yours, somewhere in Montana,
mine, in New Hampshire

that we'd travel long highways in that not knowing
still, I think that wig might be stuck on a flood fence

I think those shoes are strutting some mud bank
with attitude

alongside fishes swimming through sunheat that may
or may not have baked them into the earthly record

of all things joyful in this, our Triassic Era
our fossil history the remains still there

with the plastic bags and bones
            of the prairie dogs that scattered as we ran

they must have been coming out for a peek at us
            in the almost morning, long shadows stretching

the sun smashing in

North Valley Girls

we're north valley girls
which means we walk ditches
which means we know short cuts
which means we'll find your little brother
which means we're not afraid of goatheads

we're north valley girls
which means we know the back roads
who lives between Fourth and Second
who lives in the buffalo house on Rio Grande
whose sister got arrested by her parent's on Roehl

we're north valley girls
and we know *all* the things
like whose dad drives a one-eyed blue Chevy
where he goes when he says he's getting chicken feed
and, especially, whose mom makes the very best tortillas

we're north valley girls who know paths on acequias
we know the haunted houses and those just abandoned
we know how to leap flood fences without ripping our jackets
we know whose goat is walking there on the west side of Edith
we know all the dogs, the ones that bark and the ones that will bite

we're Alameda and Corrales
we are the Village of Los Ranchos
we're the girls from Guadalupe Trail
we're from the houses under cottonwoods
we're from ancient, sculpted fat-walled adobes

we're the girls who watch your baby
pull your weeds and water your garden
who'll let your two horses graze our front acre
we're the girls who clean the stalls, take care of the chickens

you've seen us at the State Fair with our blue ribbon
cherry pies, apple pies, plum cakes all from our family trees
We may grow up and move to El Rito, Tokyo, or New York City
but we will always be north valley girls, same ones that you remember

think of the us as the water
that moves through these fields
we're loyal   we're loyal   we're loyal

Green Chile Vs. Pandemic

a shivering protein
familiar yet strange

climbed mountains
forded streams

rode a monsoon
rode in boats

crossed an ocean
crossed a continent

shopped open markets
shopped at Wal Marts

took bullet trains
took airplanes

all to enter the house
of your chest

settle into your lungs
and multiply

gifting you
a staccato cough

oily with mucous
eyes fresh with tears

refugee, immigrant, multilingual
diverse; it came all the way

from everywhere
changed clothes

slept outside
got stuck at the border

in a cage of weeping children
separated from their parents

stopped in high Peruvian villages
delivered packages

on doorsteps
of dignitaries

climbed a thousand steps
to the country of the people

who ride minibikes
to drop off rice

finally arriving
at the small country of you

you don't complain
just cough again

while everyone you meet
hands you a mask

say they can just tell
it's plotting its next move

tomorrow
you'll go out

to hunt valley streets
and parking lots

for black dragons
with their spiced smoke

you'll wait half hour
for a hip high sack of green gold

to haul back
to the feverish kitchen of you

place on the stove
of you

stir, boil, poach, peel and spread
over the sickest days of you

sop with tortillas to swab
feverish nights

you're hoping your neighbor
was right, that in a day or two

it will help you elbow out
this intruder

chase away the ache
dissolve your fever

and guide you back
to the safe clear house

of the body
you once had, before it arrived

Dear Prehistory

I.

You sent us the pelican
and here it is, jamming with the osprey
in the lower runway of the airport.
Rummaging in the parking lot
of the pharmacy by AutoZone.
There, with the corndog wrappers
on the Jersey boardwalk.
Shuffling around like an overwrought
bride in Brooklyn.
Doing a happy merengue
with the nighthawks in Kip's Bay.
Criss-crossing golf courses, scavenging
crayfish, scrimping lizard

Stunning reminder that anywhere
on the planet is a living exhibit of history
scooping fish like pocketed silver.

II.

There are some creatures placed
on the earth just to direct us backward
in the encyclopedia of living things

And if anyone should to be assigned
to patrol those back pages
let's nominate the pelicans
who do such work every day.

Pleistocene immigrants
they throw down shadows
gargantuan as passing planes
snap whole turtles, slurp tuna
sheepshead, and crab.
They nurse their young
with their own blood.

O great midday lunacy
O omnibuses of merriment.
Darwinian evidence that dinosaurs
climbed up into the atmosphere,
throttled updrafts
dodged waterspouts, learned to
wing through ancient rains.

Nominate the pelican
for the distinction of most sturdy,
a reminder of the way
primordial atoms can calve
and combine into competent pilots
demonstrating every day
the Olympiad nature of ancestry,
the persistence of what works.

Papyrus

Once I was a piece of paper floating
down Ranchitos Road, riding a breeze

toward the intersection of Guadalupe Trail,
hooked a fence, then freed to reach North Fourth

One dimensional, hardly there
looked at from certain angles, a mere line

Sometime later, I took on doodles of birds
simple math equations

A few words I thought might make
a good country-western song

I acquired a couple dozen love letters,
a recipe for tortillas, combination lock numbers

Birthdays, so many birthdays:
sister's, daughter's, best friend's

A poem by May Sarton, a poem by Walt Whitman
Prince lyrics, Roseanne Cash, something a man I loved said

This is the truth: I spent my years
as a piece of paper blowing sideways

Destined to break down elemental –
wood pulp, water, iron, salt

Before I became everything I am
I was nothing but a place to write

Torn from a notebook
that caught on a breeze on Ranchitos Road

Making it all the way to upstate New York
I blew into the world a collection of stories

Then blowing further, I arrived back again
finally, here

the wild places

-for my riverman

let's go to the wild places
the climb-inside places

the never-before-seen places
where moonlight jumps the trees

then lies down to sleep in the grass
where sunshine circumnavigates

misshapen hills, where shadows
grey crayon their names

on the faces of canyons
let's sleep under the soft blanket

of a few million renegade stars
let's do the same wild dance they do

circling around and around
with baskets of light

life is short
so let's ride the wild rivers

sleep in the wild light
of the wild dark

I'll bring the last bit of wild in me
please, let me taste the wild of you

I Mounted the Mountains

I mounted the mountains
I fielded the fields

I rose up in arroyos
I rocked over rocks

I was bad in the badlands
I fell into the falls

I summited the summit
I was winded by wind

I sank into sinkholes
I raved in ravines

I sunbathed in sunshine
I lay in the lakes

I was revived by rivers
I muddled in mud

I foraged in forests
I coasted the coasts

I meandered the mesas
I grazed in the grass

I went wild in wilderness
I caved in the caves

I was deserted in deserts
I was swamped in the swamps

I escaped the escarpment
I was engulfed in the gulf

I holed up in the hollow
I sprang in the springs

I arched through the arches
I pondered the pond

I paid tribute to tributaries
I streamed through the streams

I ran the rapids
I researched the reef

This world smashes me daily
It loves and betrays me

It invites and then jails me
It drowns and then saves me

The End of the World

Is here. Tonight.
The sky, bruised blue-black,
is grumbling.

The ground, parched and cracked
in summer, is weeping mud,
overflowing ditches.

The arroyos are birthing
new rivers, the Rio Grande
is finally grand.

After Hermit's Peak and Calf Canyon
scarred the north, everyone, everywhere,
prayed for deluge.

Tonight, in the downpour,
the toads have come out;
in the middle of Candelaria

Someone's bloated orange tabby
floats by. "You gotta' be careful
what you wish for,"

Quips everyone
who has ever lived,
and they're right.

Tonight brought it on:
selfish, brutal, apocalyptic water.
Hail. Gnats.

Scurrying cockroaches.
In the bosque, hundred-year-old
cottonwoods, down like blown wheat

Then, as suddenly as they opened,
the windows of the sky close,
a semitruck of tangerine clouds

Drives up over the mountains,
followed by a hallelujah chorus
of rainbows.

Piled paint and splash light
stack three stories high,
pink and orange as a drunken rose bush.

Soon, the birds will return
to the pollinator tree.
I'll pick up an armful of sticks,

Build an altar to all things
ending, and all things
beginning again.

ACKNOWLEDGEMENTS

The Climate Change Chronicles (anthology)— The End of the World
Love in the Original Language (anthology) — "Wild"
Ink (27th Annual Anthology) — "Chachalaca."
Crosswinds Poetry Journal — "Papyrus", "Dear Prehistory", "Night of The Cover Bands"
Which Side Are You On (anthology) — "Labor Arbitrator"
San Antonio Review — "everything is opposite"
Blue Mesa Review — "Mermaids of Albuquerque"

ABOUT THE AUTHOR

Elizabeth Cohen is a writer who lives in Albuquerque. She is the author of the poetry collections *Bird Light*, *The Patron Saint of Cauliflower*, *Martini Tattoo*, and *The Economist's Daughter*, the memoir *The Family on Beartown Road*, and the short story collection *The Hypothetical Girl*. She holds an MFA in poetry from Columbia University.

Milton Keynes UK
Ingram Content Group UK Ltd.
UKHW051908011124
450480UK00005B/15